S0-BSI-958

DATE DUE

GAYLORD			PRINTED IN U.S.A.

THE WHIDDEN LECTURES

1. (1956) C. W. de Kiewiet: *The Anatomy of South African Misery* (1956)

2. (1957) Vijaya Lakshmi Pandit: *The Evolution of India* (1958)

3. (1958) Ronald Syme: *Colonial Élites: Rome, Spain and the Americas* (1958)

4. (1959) Charles de Koninck: *The Hollow Universe* (1960)

5. (1960) Sir George Clark: *Three Aspects of Stuart England* (1966)

6. (1961) W. F. Albright: *New Horizons in Biblical Research* (1966)

7. (1962) J. Robert Oppenheimer: *The Flying Trapeze: Three Crises for Physicists* (1964)

8. (1963) Ian T. Ramsey: *Models and Mystery* (1964)

9. (1964) David Daiches: *The Paradox of Scottish Culture: The Eighteenth Century* (1964)

10. (1965) W. Arthur Lewis: *Politics in West Africa* (London, Allen & Unwin; New York and Toronto, Oxford University Press, 1965)

11. (1966) Sir Anthony Blunt: *Picasso's Guernica* (forthcoming)

The Lectures are delivered each year in January: the second date is the year of publication, except where otherwise stated by the Oxford University Press.

THE WHIDDEN LECTURES FOR 1961

New Horizons in
Biblical Research

W. F. ALBRIGHT

Professor Emeritus, Oriental Seminary,
Johns Hopkins University

LONDON
OXFORD UNIVERSITY PRESS
NEW YORK   TORONTO
1966

Oxford University Press, Ely House, London W.1

GLASGOW NEW YORK TORONTO MELBOURNE WELLINGTON
CAPE TOWN SALISBURY IBADAN NAIROBI LUSAKA ADDIS ABABA
BOMBAY CALCUTTA MADRAS KARACHI LAHORE DACCA
KUALA LUMPUR HONG KONG

PRINTED IN GREAT BRITAIN BY
THE CAMELOT PRESS LTD.,
LONDON AND SOUTHAMPTON

FOREWORD

THE WHIDDEN LECTURES were established in 1954 by E. C. Fox, B.A., LL.D., of Toronto, the senior member of the Board of Governors, to honour the memory of a former Chancellor of McMaster University.

The Reverend Dr. Howard P. Whidden, D.D., LL.D., D.C.L., F.R.S.C., was a man of striking appearance, unusual dignity, deep Christian conviction and ready tolerance. Born in 1871 in Antigonish, Nova Scotia, where his family had settled in 1761 after three-quarters of a century's residence in New England, he attended universities in both Canada (Acadia and McMaster) and the United States (Chicago), and also served as a minister of Baptist churches in both countries (in Ontario, Manitoba, and Ohio). From 1913 to 1923 he was President of Brandon College, Manitoba, then an affiliate of McMaster University, and for part of that period (1917–21) he represented Brandon as a Member of Parliament in the Canadian House of Commons at Ottawa. He was appointed administrative head (Chancellor) of McMaster University in 1923 and in 1930 became, in a manner of speaking, its second founder when he directed its transfer from Toronto, where it had been established since 1887, to Hamilton. His broad educational outlook and effective leadership resulted in the University's burgeoning greatly in its new location, and Dr. Whidden was able to retire in 1941 with the comforting conviction that he had built both wisely and well. He died in Toronto in 1952.

The lectures on 'New Horizons in Biblical Research' were delivered by Dr. Albright in 1961. Unfortunately the health of their author did not allow him to prepare his MS. immediately for publication; hence the delay in the appearance of the printed version. McMaster University shares Dr. Albright's regret at the lapse of time, and is immensely relieved to know that he has now recovered sufficiently to be able to see the lectures through the press.

William Foxwell Albright can fairly be regarded as the doyen of Biblical archaeologists, a world-famous savant whose writings are perused and pondered wherever the history of the Holy Land is studied. He is the author of over eight hundred books and other publications and the recipient of over twenty honorary degrees. His facility with languages, both modern and ancient, and the depth and versatility of his learning equip him admirably to deal with all aspects of Biblical studies. It will be remembered that he was the first English-speaking scholar to recognize the significance of the Dead Sea Scrolls and to realize what an important mine of information they were bound to be.

For the publication of his 1961 lectures, Dr. Albright has had the invaluable assistance of Dr. C. S. Mann, of London and Baltimore. Dr. Mann has carefully gone through all the material and made sure that it is ready for the printer. To him, as to the illustrious author of these lectures, McMaster University expresses its warm appreciation. From the many inquiries it has received, it knows that there is an eager public waiting to read what Dr. Albright said some years ago on its campus. The text has been revised and brought up to date where necessary.

October 1965   E. T. SALMON,
                          Principal of University College,
                                  McMaster University.

CONTENTS

I

Archaeology and Israelite Tradition

BIBLICAL ARCHAEOLOGY IS a much wider term than Palestinian archaeology, though Palestine itself is of course central, and is rightly regarded as peculiarly the land of the Bible. But Biblical archaeology covers all the lands mentioned in the Bible, and is thus co-extensive with the cradle of civilization. This region extends from the western Mediterranean to India, and from southern Russia to Ethiopia and the Indian Ocean. Excavations in every part of this extensive area throw some light, directly or indirectly, on the Bible.

Archaeology has become increasingly scientific since the first scientific excavations were conducted in Palestine by the late Sir Flinders Petrie. Nevertheless, William Matthew Flinders Petrie was the greatest archaeological genius of modern times. He it was who first discovered the tremendous value of ordinary unpainted as well as painted pottery, for dating purposes, pottery being now used to date strata, just as the geologist uses the fossilized remains of animals and plants. Stratigraphy is one of the two indispensable pillars on which the structure of modern archaeology is erected, the other being typology, that is, the study of the forms, decorations and functions of objects made by the hand of man.

Since Petrie's time, new methods have been introduced. The Reisner-Fisher method was an attempt to survey and record everything as fully as possible by photography and drawing. This involved the exact reproduction of original location, and extensive, almost comprehensive, coverage of each stratum. Unfortunately this method has proved to be somewhat difficult of achievement. More recently, Sir Mortimer Wheeler and his pupil, Dr. Kathleen Kenyon, have developed a new method derived from the old trenching method. They have transformed the latter into an exceedingly careful, meticulously accurate study of the stratification as it appears on the vertical walls of an excavated trench. After the walls have been cleared and smoothed down as carefully as possible, everything on them is recorded—every floor level, every dump, every foundation, every stratum; and then lateral trenches are dug. This method has to be used with much more care than any previous method, but, if so used, it yields results that are far superior. It can be and has been misused. When there is nothing but a mass of stone foundations and walls, thickly bound together in apparently inextricable confusion, this method is obviously inappropriate. It is the sound combination of the two methods that is characteristic of the best excavations of our day.

Miss Kenyon has followed the new method at Jericho, where it has yielded important results. She has delved into the history of the oldest known fortified (and therefore permanent) town, going as far back as about 7000 B.C., according to a number of radio-carbon datings. Contemporary Pre-pottery Neolithic deposits are now being found in numerous places throughout the Near and Middle East. A significant recent excavation which has yielded a culture very similar to that of Jericho is that of Çatal Hüyük in south-western Asia Minor, carried out by James Mellaart in recent years. This site is at a distance of at least fifteen hundred miles by road from Jericho.

Another extremely important excavation was conducted by Yigael Yadin for four seasons (1955–8) at the North Israelite site of Hazor. With the assistance of a very large staff of over thirty archaeologists and technical experts and several hundred Israeli labourers, Professor Yadin has cleared about one four-hundredth of this great site. He has suggested that it would take eight hundred years of about four or five months work per year to clear the entire site. He and his staff are masters of Palestinian archaeology. They know the pottery, and they devote the utmost attention to studying it. Their pottery chronology is unrivalled today. Since Hazor is the most important city of Bronze Age Palestine yet touched, we can justifiably expect important, even epoch-making, results.

In the autumn of 1960, M. Jean Perrot, a French archaeologist working in Israel, uncovered the remains of a fishing and farming village, a permanent though unwalled settlement of houses with stone foundations, which had been occupied generation after generation during the Mesolithic Age, dated about 8000 B.C. This is the oldest permanent village yet found anywhere in the world.

There are a great many smaller excavations, both in Jordan and in Israel, in which scholars of many nationalities emulate one another in the hope of producing important results, so that year by year Palestinian archaeology is being developed and advanced. Increasingly we shall be able to reconstruct successive cultures, to date them within very narrow limits, and to confirm, illustrate, and correct in detail the Biblical historical tradition.

The tremendous advances that have been made in early chronology are due largely to the impact of nuclear physics on archaeology. Specifically we are indebted to Willard Libby, who in 1960 was awarded the Nobel Prize in Chemistry for his contributions to archaeology and geology. He it was who introduced the radio-carbon method of dating, which, since its introduction, has been repeatedly improved, so that we can now date back as far as 60,000 or 70,000 years, though with a rapidly increasing margin of error as we approach those figures.

There are other new discoveries which were not made in Palestine, but which are nevertheless of tremendous importance for Biblical archaeology in its wider sense; in the sense, that is, which includes the decipherment and interpretation of written objects found by the archaeologists. The use of non-written materials to elucidate the Bible is always subject to much more caution than the use of written documents. The

4

discoveries referred to consist of written materials in great quantity which have been found in four excavations outside Palestine—two in Mesopotamia, two in Syria.

Mari (modern Tell el-Hariri), situated on the middle Euphrates, has been excavated by M. André Parrot since 1933. A palace found here, dating back to the period between 1730 and 1695 B.C., i.e. the Patriarchal Age, yielded, among other things of great importance, many thousands of cuneiform tablets written by a king, his officials, and rulers of neighbouring countries, most of whom were North-Western Semites speaking a language almost identical with that of the Patriarchs. We make this latter judgement on the basis of the proto-Hebrew words, expressions, syntax, and proper names found in the texts. Thus we have here a vast amount of material which throws direct light on the antecedents of Israel in the first half of the second millennium B.C.

Another site, farther to the east, is Nuzi, where a succession of investigators, mostly American, have cleared the remains of a number of villas, as well as of the citadel of the ancient town; from these ruins they have recovered many thousands of cuneiform tablets, which illustrate a customary law so closely resembling what we find in Genesis, that it is possible to speak of the customary law of Genesis and that of Nuzi as virtually identical. All sorts of obscurities in Genesis, which are without explanation in the Hebrew text as it has come down to us, and which have remained unexplained until our time, have been clarified since

5

1925 by the tablets from Nuzi and by their interpretation.

Alalakh in northern Syria was excavated by the late Sir Leonard Woolley for several campaigns. The name of the site is not Semitic. It presumably belongs to one of the old epichoric languages, neither Semitic nor Indo-European, and as yet unidentifiable. However, this town too has yielded quantities of cuneiform tablets which illustrate the theory and practice of law among the Canaanites and their congeners and neighbours in the seventeenth and the fourteenth and fifteenth centuries B.C.

But more important than any of these places is the North Syrian port of Ugarit, modern Ras Shamra. From 1929 until the present this site has been worked by Claude Schaeffer, and has produced a wealth of materials of all kinds: art, architecture, and especially inscriptions in half a dozen languages and many scripts, predominantly Babylonian cuneiform and the native alphabetic Canaanite. Here was something undreamed of before 1931—over a thousand complete and fragmentary tablets written in an old cuneiform alphabet with twenty-seven letters (plus three others not equivalent to anything in our ancestral linear alphabet), and preserving a North-west Semitic dialect that is essentially pre-Phoenician Canaanite, which was very closely related to the Hebrew of the time of Moses. The literature thus recorded includes epics, religious texts of all kinds, letters, and economic texts. The poetic structure, style, and even the phraseology of the epics, are closely related to the same features of the oldest poetic texts of the Bible, not to mention the close correspondence of grammar and vocabulary.

The appearance of these significant written materials reminds the serious student of Biblical history, literature, and archaeology that he needs to be at home both in linguistics and in philology, linguistics being the systematic study of the languages, and philology being the interpretation of the texts. Both structural linguistics and historical linguistics are important. The former is now being applied to Biblical Hebrew by T. O. Lambdin of Harvard and his pupil, Francis Andersen. The latter consists of tracing back pronunciation, grammatical forms, etc., by comparative and historical methods. In fact, all the important results of historical Hebrew linguistics have been confirmed by the discovery of contemporary texts in North-west Semitic. But primarily, we must pursue the study of Semitic historical linguistics, because the Hebrew Bible is a literary work containing poetry and prose composed during about a thousand years from not later than the thirteenth century B.C. down to the second century B.C.

Having outlined the present state of Biblical archaeology, we shall turn to see what light archaeology has cast on a particular stage of Israelite tradition, namely, the Patriarchal traditions of Genesis. Any approach to Genesis must reckon with two clear distinctions. First, a sharp line must be drawn between the Hebrew cosmogonic and ethnogonic traditions of Genesis and those of Canaan or Phoenicia and Egypt, with whose religious traditions they have little or nothing in common. On the other hand, they indubitably come from the same stock as corresponding ancient Mesopotamian traditions. In particular, the Flood story of Genesis has many striking similarities with the parallel Sumero-Accadian stories of Mesopotamia. This means that there is good reason to believe the accuracy of the Israelite traditions which claim that their ancestors derive, in the main, from Mesopotamia, specifically from Ur of the Chaldees (excavated by Sir Leonard Woolley) and Harran (excavated in very small part by a British expedition headed by Seton Lloyd). Our other evidence confirms this tradition. The second distinction to be drawn is between the first eleven chapters of Genesis, and the rest of the book. The first eleven chapters are neither history nor theology; they are not poetry, but neither are they prose. They are in a special category of their own, which originally must have been poetic in form, and certainly had from the beginning an irreducible religious content which was never lost. These traditions were handed down from time immemorial, and gradually deepened their spiritual character as they took their final (and present) form. If we recognize the essentially religious character of the first chapter of Genesis, we can safely say that this chapter will not be easily antiquated. The extraordinary thing is that it is more evolutionary in some respects than anything published before the early nineteenth century in Europe, as far as I know.

8

The rest of Genesis contains traditions of historical character, though still of course going back to oral tradition. The significance of the latter is that oral material takes on certain fixed forms designed to ensure the preservation of features which might otherwise drop out. There were also aids to memory which were interspersed through oral compositions to draw attention to the meaningful content of words and names, and to associate a given tradition with the correct persons and places; such mnemonic aids are called aetiological.

The finds at Nuzi illuminate some of the obscurities in the customary law of Genesis.[1] Before the Nuzi tablets were published, scholars were quite unable to explain why the mysterious Eliezer of Damascus appeared as the heir of Abraham before the birth of Isaac. We now know that since, according to old Patriarchal practice, property was inalienable, a legal fiction was set up whereby, if a person had to mortgage his property because of bad harvests or rash gambling, the creditor was adopted by the debtor, whose property he inherited. We may conjecture that this Eliezer was a rich Damascene merchant who, like Damascene merchants ever since, lent money to the surrounding peasants and nomads, by whom he had himself adopted.[2]

[1] The best collection of Nuzi parallels to the Old Testament material is in E. A. Speiser's *Genesis* (New York, 1964), based as it is on a knowledge of Nuzi material unequalled by any other modern scholar.

[2] This particular parallel was not fully used by Speiser, owing to his contention that there was no trace of customs of adoption in Israel. This view is now known to be incorrect, and a forthcoming study by one of Speiser's pupils will illustrate both the practice and the terms

Another odd story tells of Rachel's stealing her father's household gods, his 'teraphim', and sitting on them so that Laban's search proved useless. In the Nuzi texts, when there is doubt about an inheritance, for instance if there is no valid will, *prima facie* evidence for right of inheritance is possession of the family gods. The Genesis passage itself offers no explanation of the incident: it has simply been handed down by one editor after another, none knowing what it meant, but all loath to cut it out in case it might have some real significance. These are just two examples of the many mysteries in Genesis that are being solved by the discoveries at Nuzi and elsewhere.

Today, therefore, nearly all Biblical scholars are coming to recognize that the stories of Genesis go back to very ancient oral traditions. These oral traditions dramatize. They omit historical details that the modern historian would like to have. But they preserve details of literary and religious significance, so that their value for pedagogical purposes is very much greater than it would have been if they had just described wars, movements of tribes, genealogies and so on.

If the customary law of Genesis is a faithful reflection of contemporary law, if the social and legal practices recorded in Genesis are correct for the Patriarchal Age but not for the post-Mosaic period, it follows that we cannot *a priori* dismiss the religious content of the

used in connexion with adoption in later parts of the Old Testament. This particular interpretation of Eliezer was first proposed by the present writer, and accepted by Cyrus H. Gordon and many others.

Patriarchal narratives as late. These narratives are not retrojections from the age of the Prophets, but actual oral tradition, modified only slightly in the course of time—modified, that is, by the omission of mythical elements, by the heightening of certain elements regarded as important, etc.—but still generally valid as records of early periods. Thus, though we cannot write history in the modern sense directly from the book of Genesis, we can describe the general way of life and give a rough sequence of events.[1]

One of the major contributions of archaeology has been in the area of Hebrew versification. In a number of old poems found in Genesis, Exodus, Numbers, Deuteronomy, Judges, and Psalms we find an altogether disproportionate number of survivals of ancient Canaanite style, imagery, and language as found in the Ugaritic epics. The latter were written down in their present form early in the fourteenth

[1] On the early patriarchal age, cf. especially *Bulletin of the American Schools of Oriental Research*, 163 (1961), pp. 36–54, and also the writer's *The Biblical Period from Abraham to Ezra*, Harper Torch Book (New York, 1963), pp. 1 ff. There will be further material in the author's forthcoming Jordan Lectures (University of London) for 1965 (*Canaan, Phoenicia and Israel*) to be published by McGraw-Hill. Recent attempts to telescope the patriarchal and Mosaic periods, dating Abraham about 1400 and the Exodus about 1200, are quite unnecessary. Ancient and modern Arab genealogies, together with similar examples from Rhodesia, Hawaii, as well as from many other places, usually start with the putative ancestors of the clan. After several generations there are long gaps, followed by the latest ten generations or so—the generations in between are omitted without explanation. Historical analogy suggests that the same may be true of the Biblical genealogies, and that in fact, as all our other evidence indicates, there was an interval of several centuries between the earliest patriarchal period and the time of Moses.

century B.C., well before the time of Moses, but were copied from oral compositions of considerably earlier date. Frequently the poetic structure is the same in both the Ugaritic epics and these old Biblical poems. The same is true of pairs of words, nearly a hundred of which appear in both literatures. Also in the Biblical poems are many mythological allusions drawn from the literature of the surrounding Canaanite and non-Israelite Hebrew-speaking areas. The latter are, however, literary reminiscences and indeed in some cases have later become transformed, particularly in the Psalter.

From the materials now available it is possible to set up a sequence-dating of Hebrew poetry. Just as in Old and Middle English literature, in early Greek and Roman poetry, Assyrian cuneiform and Egyptian hieroglyphic literature, we can see how one style gives way to another, so also we can discover in Hebrew poetry a changing sequence of styles, and from this sequence we can determine the relative age of the poems in question. Earliest is the Song of Miriam (Exod. 15), which, though somewhat later than the early Canaanite poetic literature of a comparable type, is in many ways almost identical with it in structure. Closely related to it is the Song of Deborah, followed by the Oracles of Balaam, in part if not entirely. Later come the Blessing of Moses (Deut. 33), the Song of Moses (Deut. 32), and the Blessing of Jacob (Gen. 49). Further, through the books of Exodus and Numbers, and to some extent in Joshua, we have brief early poetic quotations which clearly reflect the same kinds of poetic style as we have in these longer poems. Such poetic reminiscences provide a very valuable check on the antiquity of the stories in which they are embedded, most of which go back to poetic originals coming from the thirteenth or twelfth centuries B.C.[1]

The Mosaic period also has been considerably illuminated by archaeology. Of course, no reference to Moses has been found in any excavated document; it would be extremely surprising if one ever were found. Only a tiny proportion of all the important Egyptians and Semites living in Egypt during the thirteenth century B.C. are mentioned in any documentary source. And Moses is particularly unlikely to be mentioned, because his importance is not related in any way to Egypt but solely to the future Israel. He was the founder of Israel, including its religion, law, culture, statehood. Israel had to have a founder. Nowhere in history is there an example of such unique institutions growing up out of nothing by a process that cannot be defined, because of supposed lack of documentary attestation.

From the early poetry of which we have spoken— full-length poems, shorter poems and poetic reminiscences, even a few single lines of verse—it is possible to write a sketch of Mosaic history which would in general confirm the prose account which has come down to us. In fact, the poetic version sometimes preserves a fuller record. For example, the prose traditions recorded in

[1] This will be further dealt with in Chapter I of the above-mentioned Jordan Lectures.

the 14th chapter of Exodus and the 4th chapter of Judges can only be understood, historically speaking, from the poetic accounts in the 15th and 5th chapters of the respective books. Though the Oracles of Balaam and the Song of Miriam were probably not written down for the first time until the tenth century, they certainly had a long oral transmission, deriving for the most part from Israel's beginnings. We thus have a solid background for Israelite tradition, which is quite independent of later editorial work on J, E, D, etc.

Much of the source-analysis of modern critical scholarship from the school of Wellhausen on has been based on the erroneous notion that the consonantal text, and often even the vowels of the Pentateuch, remained completely unchanged after a supposed final redaction about the fifth century B.C., perhaps under Ezra. However, we now know that there were many different textual recensions in the following period. Examination of the Dead Sea Scrolls and renewed study of the Septuagint have brought concrete evidence that the Massoretic tradition was only one of a number, and that the consonantal text of the Pentateuch as known in all Hebrew manuscripts up to recent years as well as in all printed Hebrew Bibles, is by no means the same as it was when these documents were originally written and compiled. Consequently the attempt to break a text down into minute units, sometimes sharing a single verse, even a short verse, among three different sources, is quite futile. But although these fundamentalist 'higher critics' are quite wrong in their presuppositions, it does not necessarily follow that the documentary hypothesis in general is wrong. But it does have to be treated with much more critical circumspection than has hitherto been the case.

What was Moses' place in history? By comparing the cultic, ritual, and civil legislation of the Pentateuch with earlier and later developments, we can show that it must come in the middle—somewhere between the fourteenth and eleventh centuries B.C. It fits nowhere else. Similarly we can show that the religion of the Pentateuch after Genesis is intermediate between Patriarchal religion on the one hand, and the religion of the Monarchy on the other, and so must be Mosaic in our broad sense. Consequently Moses must have been a monotheist—not, of course, a philosophical monotheist, since it is quite impossible to speak of philosophy in any technical sense before the emergence of Greek philosophy with Thales and his successors between the beginning of the sixth century B.C. and the late fourth century B.C. There is no philosophy as such in the Hebrew Bible. However, there is much serious thinking —certainly sufficient raw material for modern scholars to draw up an approximate creed.

Because the Bible knows no philosophical schematization, we should not expect abstract accounts of institutions. Frank Cross has shown that the references to the tabernacle between Sinai and Samuel reflect different stages in its history.[1] One might compare the British constitution, which contains elements from a

[1] See the article by F. M. Cross in *The Biblical Archaeologist*, 10 (1947).

great many different periods and is still a changing, growing institution. Yet in pre-philosophical times it would have been described as monolithic. Even today the American constitution is conceived in this sense by the ordinary man. And indeed it is an organic unity; yet it is composed of the original 1789 constitution, an ever-increasing number of amendments, and many new interpretations of words, legal usages, and implications so that the constitution as understood today is far from identical with the constitution as understood in 1789. So with the tabernacle. The tabernacle of the priestly source represents the last stage of development, dating possibly from the time of Samuel but more likely from the time of David. But many references to the tabernacle are obviously much more archaic, going back to the time of Moses. The account fails to distinguish between successive stages of the institution—a natural feature of pre-philosophical thought.

By taking such facts as these into account, we may eliminate many of the supposed contradictions and difficulties.

2

The Ancient Israelite mind in its Environmental Context[1]

THERE ARE MANY commonly held views about the Bible which are at worst quite erroneous, at best subject to much study and eventual correction. For instance it is often said that Old Testament thought is primitive, and therefore irrelevant to modern man. The Israelites knew nothing of modern science or philosophy: their thinking was kept within the confines of the terms and thought-patterns of primitive humanity, and holds nothing of value for modern thought. Another very common misconception is that Biblical thought is oriental and exotic, and consequently of no significance for the western mind; and presumably of no significance for the modern oriental mind, which has in the interim been, or is in the process of being, westernized.

A major area of discussion concerns the relationship between ancient Israelite and Hellenic ways of thinking. It has been claimed that the Israelites were quite philosophically minded—for example, in a very eloquent book entitled *The Hebrew Philosophical Genius* by Duncan Macdonald, a distinguished Arabist, famous in his time as an authority on Islamic religion,

[1] Cf. also Chapter 3 of the author's *History, Archaeology and Christian Humanism* (New York, 1965), pp. 83–100.

law, and history. The book was reviewed by George Boas, a keen analytic philosopher, who pointed out that the Israelites did not ask the questions that philosophers ask, nor did they answer the questions they did ask as philosophers do. In other words, there is no technical philosophy, or anything approaching it, anywhere in the Old Testament.

There is a strong tendency today to go too far in the opposite direction, and to contrast Israelite ways of thinking with Greek thought in such a way as to create a maximal psychological and logical difference between the two. The most important expression of this tendency is a learned book by Thorlief Boman: *Das hebräische Denken in Vergleich mit dem griechischen*.[1] This is an elaborate study, based on full knowledge of the relevant literature. I believe that Boman is wrong on all essential points, but this does not affect the impact of his work.

One example of the distinctions drawn by this school of thought is that the Hebrews were 'ear-minded', the Greeks 'eye-minded'. This would seem to be entirely baseless, since probably all physiologists and psychologists would admit that the proportion of auditory to visual thinking is roughly the same in all races. It may eventually be found that there are some elements of racial psychology which do vary; but they are so elusive that no means of measuring them has yet been found.

A second distinction that Boman, for example,

[1] English translation: *Hebrew Thought Compared with Greek*, London, 1960.

accepts, is old: Hebrew thinking was dynamic, whereas Greek was static. An illustration is the use of the words for 'to be' in the two languages. The ordinary word for 'to be' in Hebrew, *hāyāh*, means generally 'to become', although really neither word is a good translation of *hāyāh*. In Greek, *einai* is 'to be'. It does not mean 'become', for which there is a special word, *gignesthai*. From this it is concluded that *hāyāh* is dynamic, while *einai* is static. The difficulty with this is that in Hebrew one may also say, *'anî hû'*, 'I am', using the pronoun. In actual fact the Greeks had as much freedom in expressing the idea 'become' as the Hebrews, and the Hebrews were just as capable of expressing the idea 'be' as the Greeks, the only difference being that they did not use the same syntactical devices. No more valid are the views of von Dobschütz and Cullmann, who have claimed that Hebrew thought was temporal, Greek thought spatial.

Such distinctions do of course exist, but among individuals, not nations or races. Unfortunately the specialists who subscribe to the doctrines mentioned have substituted mere wordplay for rigorous sorting and evaluation of evidence.

Now I am far from denying the importance of language in thinking. Not for nothing has French been used as the language of diplomacy for several centuries. In general, it is a very precise language. (And yet one member of the Académie Française has caused considerable indignation by suggesting that it is beginning to lose that precision.) German has special advantages and disadvantages in its system of compound words. Any two, sometimes three, nouns can be combined to form a new compound word, with a meaning different from the sum of its components and often introducing wholly new overtones. In this way the Germans are able to develop all sorts of metaphysical nuances, which are much more difficult in English, and impossible in French without circumlocution. But this does not mean that these ideas cannot be expressed in English or French. It does mean that German metaphysical thinking is less precise, more inclined to vagueness, and consequently very difficult, though not impossible, to translate. Thus Hegelian and existentialist systems have passed out of German-speaking countries into English- and French-speaking countries without losing any essential features.

This brings us to consider the structural and semantic approach to linguistic psychology. It is associated in America with the name of the late Count Alfred Korzybski, founder of the so-called semantic school, to which many Americans and Britons fell prey. The best popular works on the subject are by S. Hayakawa, a Japanese-American professor of English, and Thurman Arnold. These men have made a valuable contribution by pointing out the tyranny of words in an unilingual culture. (In a bi- or trilingual culture there is much more freedom from this tyranny because people are used to expressing the same idea in different languages.) But while it is true that basic modes of thinking are nationally and culturally conditioned, it does not follow that they reflect a peculiar racial or linguistic psychology, as these men claim.

Benjamin Lee Whorf was a brilliant American engineer who wrote on a wide range of subjects. In particular he published a series of articles on linguistic psychology which soon became classics. His ideas were in fact highly original, and convinced many. However, they were almost entirely wrong. (Of course, initial mistakes often lead to great discoveries: by recognizing a mistake one may be able to bypass it in later thought.) Whorf tried to construct completely different systems of logical thinking on the basis of different linguistic structures. He claimed, for instance, that since Navajo has a unique structure, it must therefore have a system of thinking totally different from that of any other language, and consequently a unique logic. The way in which he proceeded is unbelievable to one trained in both structural and historical linguistics. He took Navajo sentences, distinguished all the formative elements, prefixes, suffixes, and so on, and gave them what he thought was the correct original etymology. But we do not know the etymology of formative elements (morphemes) in languages far better known and longer studied than Navajo, for example that of the initial *ge* and final *ing* (*ung*) in the Germanic languages. Such elements have long prehistories which we cannot trace, speech being as old as true tool-making, which goes back at least 200,000 years according to the latest work of Emiliani. Benjamin Lee Whorf's etymologies of morphemes are quite unreliable. Consequently the supposed logical distinctions which he based on them are equally arbitrary.

There are, accordingly, no basic logical differences between languages. There are simply minor differences in the things expressed, and minor differences in the ways of expressing things. For the former we need only compare primitive with modern man. Each talks about things the other may not have heard of. This does not mean that the two have different logics: it means merely that they are exposed to, and interested in, different things. For the latter we may again compare Hebrew and Greek. In Hebrew and other Semitic languages there is a specific verbal form to express causation, formed by adding a simple prefix to the root, and used as naturally as we use an active or a passive form. Thus causation was embedded in the structure of the language: there was nothing abstract about the idea. And yet it was the Greeks who first developed the philosophical notion of causation—though their language had nothing in its structure which enabled them to express the concept simply and directly. The obvious conclusion is that the structure of a language does *not* determine the logic of the people speaking that language.

I propose the historical approach to the problem of ways of thinking in antiquity as far more reliable than any supposed psychological or logical approach. In the early part of this century, a French psychologist by the name of Lévy-Bruhl devoted himself to the study of anthropological and ethnological literature, and concluded that there were two main stages of thinking, one of which he called pre-logical, and the other of which he called logical. The pre-logical was in his opinion the mentality of primitives, by which he meant savages of today and primitives of prehistoric times. His work *La mentalité primitive* was in its time considered epoch-making, and, in my opinion, still is, even though, just before the beginning of the Second World War, Lévy-Bruhl began to think over the objections raised against his views by other anthropologists, and in his famous *Carnets*, first published posthumously in 1947 in the *Revue Philosophique* and then later in book form, he concluded that he had been wrong and retracted his view. Although he had no difficulty in proving that the primitive mind did not take into account abstract causation, was not conscious of basic differences between animals and men, and did not know the logical principles of identity and contradiction, yet he had to admit that if a primitive is sent out as a tracker or hunter or fisher, he is more logical than a modern European would be if put into the same situation— because he knows his environment. It is a logic born of experience, but it is as thorough-going as any Greek logic. So Lévy-Bruhl was quite right in admitting that within limits primitive man was strictly logical, long before the birth of Greek logic.

We must look more closely at this primitive logic. The man of the ancient Near East developed a rigorously logical approach to many everyday occupations, to ordinary law and social practice, as well as to the arts and crafts. Thousands of years ago man had already invented innumerable devices and gadgets, processes and uses of materials—many of which were subsequently lost and often remain so today. Others have been rediscovered after decades of effort on the part of modern technicians. Many chemists, ceramists, and archaeologists have spent a large part of their lives trying to make Attic black-figured or red-figured glaze. Only now are we beginning to rediscover some of the inventions of ancient men.

Coming to Lévy-Bruhl's books after intensive study of the history of ancient science and technology, I saw that there were important distinctions to be drawn within the material illustrating ancient mentality. We certainly have in ancient Near Eastern religion, mythology, magic, and indeed in most higher culture, that same failure to distinguish logical relations which Lévy-Bruhl found among modern primitives. This had been noted by G. van der Leeuw and others as far back as the twenties, but their work had not been followed up. Before 1940, I distinguished among three stages of logic. The first I called originally pre-logical, following Lévy-Bruhl. The term is not satisfactory, because it is not simply a chronological category. It is distinguished rather by an inability to control, by ordinary everyday human experience, dream life, religious phenomena, phenomena of magic and art, etc. Consequently, I soon adopted the term proto-logical instead of pre-logical.

But that part of Lévy-Bruhl's pre-logical category which he subsequently found to be not pre-logical at all,

I termed empirico-logical—that is, a logic based on experience. The third category is of course formal logic.

These three categories can best be illustrated by an historical survey of the literature of the Near East. In the whole of ancient Near Eastern literature there is not one instance of Greek logic, not a single syllogism. This is also true of the Homeric epics as well as of Hesiod and the early lyric poets. The earliest literatures in the Near East are those of Egypt, Babylonia, Assyria, Asia Minor, Phoenicia, etc. Most of the true literary material from these cultures precedes the twelfth century—comparatively little is later. (This does not include royal inscriptions or business documents, many of which are, of course, later.) With very few notable exceptions, this ancient oriental literature is proto-logical in character. The next stage is represented by the Hebrew Bible, the literature of which I should date almost entirely between 1300 B.C. and 400 B.C., though there is a little that comes down to the second century B.C. It is thus later than most canonical writings of the pagan Near East chronologically. It also follows them logically, since it is almost all empirico-logical, only occasionally proto-logical.[1]

Greek literature, with the notable exception of

[1] Proto-logical intuition cannot, however, be ultimately separated from experience, since it is the result of subconscious mental processes combining, in a way which cannot yet be described, different deposits of knowledge, stored away as memory, and deriving originally from sense-experience and reflection. We think that it is something new only because we are not aware of its origin. That it must grow out of previous experience is illustrated by the fact that only the trained mathematician will have flashes of mathematical intuition.

25

Homer and Hesiod, dates after about 700 B.C. It began after the bulk of Hebrew literature was completed. The importance of the chronological factor in comparing Greek and Hebrew literatures may be further illustrated by considering the prose of the two languages. Our earliest Greek prose fragments, omitting inscriptions, date from the sixth century B.C. The earliest literary monument of prose is the work of Herodotus, from the late fifth century B.C., who was thus almost contemporary with the last historian of Israel, the Chronicler. Almost all the historical writing in the Old Testament was completed generations before Herodotus. So when we compare Greek historical writing in its fresh vigour in the fifth century with the last survivals of a Hebrew historical writing that had flourished generations earlier, we pre-judge the issue.

It has been claimed that Greek philosophical thinking has markedly influenced parts of the Old Testament, especially Job and Ecclesiastes. I should date Job roughly in the seventh century B.C. While it is profound in its insights and in the problems it raises, there is no trace of a Greek philosophical treatment of those problems. Ecclesiastes may now be dated with confidence (as will be shown elsewhere) in the Persian period, probably in the late fifth century B.C. But although I recognize community of thinking between the Preacher and much Greek thinking of the sixth century B.C., as well as with the Phoenician material which we possess from this general period, I cannot see any trace of Greek philosophical thinking as many, including myself, once did.

Hebrew literature is thus older than comparable Greek literature. Nowhere previous to the sixth century —neither in the pagan Near East nor in the Old Testament, nor in Homer, Hesiod or the lyric poets of early Greek literature—can any trace of true philosophical thinking be found.

For years I have been intensively engaged in studying the Greek shift to philosophical abstraction and logical thought which began with Thales and Anaximander.[1] How did Greek thinkers become philosophers and logicians? We have already said that there was no philosophy nor logical thinking before Thales and Anaximander, and these two were universally considered by the later Greeks themselves to have been the first philosophers. They undoubtedly drew very heavily on older empirical knowledge, both native and taken from the East; they learned to derive general principles from empirical data. Thales is said to have drawn up the first list of geometrical propositions or theorems. Some scholars insist that he demonstrated his theorems by later Greek syllogistic methods, but there is no evidence at all to prove this. Most specialists on the history of Greek logic and philosophy consider that the method of demonstrating geometrical theorems which we associate with Euclid, developed first in a more

[1] See especially a discussion of the factors involved in the Greek intellectual revolution in my forthcoming *Experience on the Road to Reason*, to be published by McGraw-Hill.

archaic form in the course of the fifth century B.C. on the basis of foundations laid in the sixth or seventh. But the theorems themselves had to be set up, before their correctness could be demonstrated by logical processes.

Now we can trace, stage by stage, the development of law in the ancient Near East from the early case system to increasing use of generalized principles. Thales, who, according to Herodotus, was a leading constitutional lawyer, and who was interested in everything, scientific and human, must have been familiar with the codified case law of the ancient Orient and of seventh-century Greece. He may well have collected what he could find of ancient oriental mathematical problems (in the case form in which the mathematics of Babylonia, Egypt, etc., appears). Following the pattern developing in law, he would then have grouped cases together, generalized them, and so first produced propositions or theorems. They could not yet be demonstrated, but they would be stated, and correctly stated. In itself such generalization was a tremendous advance; it is also what we must expect in the emergence of Greek philosophy and logic.

I have said that the Old Testament is a monument of empirical logic. I shall proceed to illustrate this statement. First, the development of law shows the influence of Israel's empirical logic. Nowhere in Babylonian or Hittite law do we find generalizing propositions. We see rather from the half-dozen cuneiform collections of laws which we possess, that each law is a specialized case or cluster of cases. The so-called Book of the

Covenant (Exodus 21–23) belongs typologically with the cuneiform laws though it shows clear traces of later revision. Mosaic law takes these earlier laws for granted, it presupposes them. Many formulae, and sometimes whole laws, are identical word for word (allowing of course for the difference in languages) with parallel matter in the Code of Hammurapi and the Eshnunna code. But the Mosaic legislation takes us a stage farther. For the first time in history, we find a series of general laws: the Ten Commandments. Unfortunately for the historian, their exact date is not certain, though their original formulation cannot be later than the tenth century B.C., and may easily go back to the thirteenth. (In later times slightly differing forms appear, two in the Old Testament itself, and others in different recensions, as we know from the Greek translation and the Nash Papyrus.)

The Lex Talionis (Exodus 21.23–25), 'life for life, eye for eye', is the oldest known explicit statement of a fundamental legal principle, equal justice for all. Today it may sound harsh, but it was a tremendous improvement over earlier vendetta law or differential penalties depending on the social status of aggressor and victim.

Such generalized formulations take us a step beyond empirical logic in the direction of generalization, though they never quite reach the Greek level. Their degree of generalization is slightly more advanced than that of generalizing cases.

Another phase of culture illustrating the advance of empirical logic in the Hebrew Bible is poetry. In ancient

Near Eastern poetry, there is a tendency to place in parallelism statements that defy the principle of identity. This is particularly common in the pre-Israelite poetry of Palestine and Syria, an abundance of which has been recovered in the course of the excavations at Ugarit; but it also occurs in the very earliest Biblical poetry. In the Song of Deborah, which is very close in style to the preceding Canaanite or North-west Semitic poetry, we read that Jael, the courageous woman who killed the Canaanite Sisera after the defeat of his army by the Israelites, seized

> 'a tent-peg with her hand,
> a mallet with her right hand',

and hammered the head of Sisera (Judges 5.26). Later they understood it literally (in the prose account of chapter 4 of Judges) and explained that what Jael actually did was to take the tent-peg in one hand, place it on Sisera's temple while he slept, then take the mallet in the other and with it drive the peg through his skull. Actually, as we know from numerous stylistic parallels in Canaanite literature, the poetic account means merely that she took peg and hammer and smashed his head with both, without wasting time or risking his waking up while she first put the peg into position.

Thus, though such proto-logical thinking did not disturb the earliest Israelites, it soon became quite foreign to them, and the rest of Hebrew poetry is thoroughly empirico-logical.

History is another area in which we can see Israel's intellectual growth. The first real history found anywhere in the ancient Near East is in the book of Samuel, especially the famous court history, extending from David's succession to the throne in 2 Samuel to his death at the beginning of 1 Kings. The latter is an extraordinary document; it is almost history in the modern sense, and quite similar to the kind of history that Herodotus wrote, though Herodotus had a speculative and philosophical approach that is quite absent from the Hebrew Bible. But historical Hebrew narrative also lacks the speculations and dubious analogies with which Herodotus abounds, coming after a century and a half of speculative thought. Here early Israel's empirical logic has produced something unique in its way. Her best historical writing far outshines Herodotus in sobriety and realism.

The empirical logic of the Hebrew Bible also appears in Israel's religion. In Bronze Age Palestine and Syria there was a continual fluctuation of sex, function, and identity among the gods, as we know from the rich literature now at our disposal. The principle of contradiction is flouted at every turn. It is quite inappropriate to ask: how did the God of nature become the God of ethics in Israel?—because the god of nature was also lord of ethics from remote pre-Israelite times. In Assyria and Babylonia the sun-god was also patron of justice, and there was a similar relation in the case of all high gods. Proto-logical polytheisms did not make a logical distinction between nature and ethics.

31

The confusion of identity between divinities, as well as the internal contradictions of every kind which characterized pagan mythologies, were intolerable to empirico-logical Israel. They did not ring true to her experience. Leaving on one side the question of revelation, we may be sure that when men began to consider nature seriously and to see the contradictions and absurdities in the polytheisms around them, they were almost certain to arrive eventually at a simple monotheistic system in which these inconsistencies were resolved. I am not suggesting that the emergence of monotheism was solely a logical process: it had to grow out of experience as well; indeed, once the idea had arisen, other aspects of monotheism would follow as its natural concomitants in an empirico-logical higher culture.

In concluding my survey of the empirical logic of the Old Testament I shall limit myself to the principle of demythologizing. *Entmythologisierung* is a term introduced by Rudolf Bultmann, but used by him in a misleading way, in my opinion. For him, it is *our* task to demythologize—we have to interpret the 'myths' of the Bible by replacing their symbols by concepts acceptable to our own philosophy. But the Bible has already 'demythologized' its source material by excising myths or by taking certain mythical elements in their corresponding empirical form, and using them in the service of a higher religious vision. It is quite absurd to claim, as he does, that New Testament Christianity presupposes a three-storey universe, because no educated man believed any more than we do in a three-storey universe or any other multi-storey universe. It is just as incongruous to say that the New Testament (or rabbinic literature or the Old Testament) is mythological because God and heaven are depicted as being 'up', as it is to say that a person believes in a geocentric universe because he speaks of the sun rising in the east and setting in the west. Nor are contemporary theologians necessarily speaking in mythological terms when they call religion 'the dimension of depth'.

In Genesis, and in some of the poetry of the Bible, there are a number of cases where mythical elements have clearly been demythologized. For example, in Canaanite mythology there was a great monster known as *tannîn*, translated 'whale' in the Authorized Version of the Bible. A *tannîn* was one of the prehistoric monsters who antedated even the gods, and who were destroyed by the great god Baal, or by his sister Anath or some other Canaanite divinity. In Genesis we are told that on the fifth day of creation God created the *tannînîm gedôlîm*, the primordial monsters of chaos. They were thus not pre-divine; they did not antedate Yahweh: they were his creations. The process of demythologization has already taken place. There are only a few traces of earlier mythology in the first chapter of Genesis, and all have been thoroughly demythologized. We should not be justified in supposing, for example, that *tehôm*, the great deep of Genesis 1, is a monster by that name, as Tihâmtu was in earlier Canaanite

33

mythology. Such allusions no more indicate belief in the reality of the original bearers of the names, than does our use of the word 'cereal' express faith in the goddess Ceres. The Bible uses a number of names of ancient gods and goddesses as common nouns. Astarte has become 'sheep-breeding'; Shulman, the god of healing, has become 'good health'; another deity has given his name to the oak-tree; another to the terebinth; another to wine. These are all instances of demythologizing.

Today we probably have as much proto-logical thinking as ancient and modern primitives, possibly more. We also have as much empirical thinking. But when we follow intellectual leadership (usually in school) we become logical in the Greek sense of the term. Even then we still do most of our thinking with our emotions. We scarcely bother with logic at all, and so we are really no different from the ancients.

Human mentality tends to offer the same universal characteristics. It is the tools men use which differ. By experience men learned to use new tools, not only in their manual labour, not only in their social life, but also in their thinking. Finally they passed the empirical stage and learned to use the tools of logical thought. Incidentally, they also opened the way for all sorts of unfortunate consequences, for while we may gain by every advance of civilization, we also suffer. Today, logical thinking is more dangerous than ever. Marxism, which is developed by an ostensibly logical form of Hegelian dialectic reasoning, is based on an artificial structure of postulates and assumptions, many of which would be accepted by few. It is the apparent solidity of the logical superstructure that has convinced a great many of the correctness of conclusions which ultimately derive from thoroughly defective postulates. If we made proper use of empirical logic, that substructure would never be constructed. So it is with most of our modern ideologies.

The Old Testament preserves a monument of human thinking which will never be superseded.

3

New Testament Research after the Discovery of the Dead Sea Scrolls

THIS TREATMENT OF the effect of the Dead Sea Scrolls on New Testament research presupposes a knowledge of the finding of the Scrolls from 1947 onwards, and of their nature and general content. I shall refer to details of their content only in so far as they pertain to the problems under discussion.

What was the state of New Testament studies at the time when the Scrolls first appeared? I refer to the situation as found in our leading universities and theological seminaries, where trained scholars often go far beyond the point where they should stop. The result is that in many instances they have to retrace their steps, while ordinary people stay where they are without having to change much at all—as is generally true in most fields. It is true of the sciences, especially the social sciences. It is true of the humanities. And it is supremely true of Biblical studies, because no other humanistic study is so deeply connected with the spiritual life and tradition of western mankind, and indeed of the whole world.

At the beginning of the year 1949, before any of the Scrolls had been published, but when people already knew something of what might be coming, the following positions were maintained by nearly all trained New Testament scholars, varying, of course, with different degrees of caution, or recklessness, but roughly representing the general consensus.

First, no original Jewish literature in Hebrew or Aramaic was known from between the book of Daniel, which seems to have been finally edited about 167 B.C., and the Scroll of Fasting, *Megillat Ta'anit*, which dates from the reign of Hadrian, about 130–135 A.D. It was therefore impossible to determine objectively the Hebrew-Aramaic background of the New Testament. The only indications were survivals of traditions that may have dated from some time within that period. Now we have a mass of datable Jewish religious literature from various times throughout that period.

Second, it was very difficult to date the intertestamental literature, comprising the Apocrypha (meaning of course books 'stored away', not forged nor fictitious documents) and the Pseudepigrapha (referring to books falsely attributed to worthies like Enoch and Moses). The Apocrypha are those books in the Greek Jewish Bible, which were never included in the Hebrew Bible. Both categories are preserved only in Greek or Ethiopic or other translations.[1] The dates that were proposed for these works before 1949 have now been shown to be largely wrong. For example, the Book of Tobit was commonly dated in the second

[1] English translations, with introduction and commentary, in R. H. Charles (ed.), *The Apocrypha and Pseudepigrapha of the Old Testament in English* (Oxford, 2 vols., 1913, reissued 1963: Vol. I *The Apocrypha*, Vol. II *The Pseudepigrapha of the Old Testament*).

or even the first century B.C., only a few scholars thinking that it might conceivably be earlier. We now have
fragmentary remains of the original Tobit in quite
a number of copies from Cave IV at Qumran. It
transpires that the Aramaic of Tobit is older than that
of Daniel in the Hebrew Bible, and virtually identical
with that of Ezra. In other words, it is the Aramaic of
the Persian Empire, the so-called Imperial Aramaic
of the fifth and fourth centuries B.C. Therefore the Book
of Tobit goes back almost certainly to the fourth, and
possibly to the fifth century B.C.—much earlier than
we had supposed. Jubilees and the Testaments of
the Twelve Patriarchs are almost certainly much older
than was supposed by R. H. Charles, C. C. Torrey,
and other recent scholars in the twentieth century,
who dated them towards the end of the second century
B.C. or even later. Thus our new material throws light
on the original languages and the dates of composition
of the intertestamental literature.

Another area of study which had reached an impasse
in 1949 was research on the language of the Greek New
Testament. From the 1890's on, many discoveries were
made in Egypt of papyrus documents, written in a
dialect very similar to that of the New Testament,
that is, in *koinē* Greek of the Hellenistic–Roman period.
Some scholars, such as the late Adolf Deissmann,
thought that this was actually the exact language of
the New Testament. But such a great authority on Hellenistic literature as the late Arthur Darby Nock,
pointed out many times in the recent past that, while

the Greek of the New Testament is *koinē* Greek, not classical Greek, it is at the same time a peculiar kind of *koinē* Greek. It is in fact the language of Jews whose native tongues were Hebrew and Aramaic, and whose Greek was often quite saturated with Hebrew and Aramaic influence, as can now be abundantly illustrated from the Scrolls. The problem of the nature of the language of the New Testament was in fact only partially solved by the discovery that the morphology of its verbs and nouns, divergent from classical Greek tradition, was actually the ordinary spoken and written Greek of that period.

Many scholars, especially the late C. C. Torrey, maintained that some of the books of the New Testament were translations of original Aramaic documents, or at least had been written by men who thought in Aramaic, and were simply writing down in Greek an Aramaic oral tradition. Torrey's views were rejected by nearly all New Testament scholars who followed the Greek tradition, but a controversy has arisen concerning the proportion of Jewish elements in the New Testament. The best known representatives of the two positions today are perhaps Rudolf Bultmann,[1] who emphasizes the Greek elements at the expense of the Jewish, and Frederick Grant,[2] who insists on the Jewishness of the New Testament. It was formerly impossible to solve this problem, because no one could

---

[1] The best all-round picture of Bultmann's thought in this connexion is to be found in his *Theology of the New Testament*, London, 1952.
[2] Cf. F. C. Grant, *The Gospels*, New York, 1959.

prove that the original language was not Greek, even though it did not always agree linguistically with the nearest Greek known, which was a quasi-literary *koinē*. Nor could anyone prove that it was not Hebrew or Aramaic, since it is quite likely that the earliest post-Christian writings of Judaism represented traditions going back at least to the time of Christ; and the inter-testamental literature, as we have seen, could not itself be fixed historically. There were simply no *points de repère*, no fixed pegs which would enable one to determine dates or relationships with ideas or data in the New Testament. This does not of course affect the religious values of the New Testament, but it does affect our understanding of its place in the history of thought and religion.

The New Testament, according to many scholars, exhibits pronounced gnostic features, and in fact is unintelligible, historically speaking, unless understood against a gnostic background. Gnostics believed that salvation came through esoteric mysteries, 'gnosis', a mysterious, superhuman, enigmatic knowledge, which was hidden from ordinary men. Now these scholars claimed that there was a pre-Christian gnosticism, and that this is best illustrated by the books of the Mandaeans, the so-called Christians of John the Baptist, who still survive in Iraq on the lower Tigris. This is rather a surprising claim, since, although John the Baptist is their great hero, the Mandaeans consider Jesus as their great demon or devil, and are bitterly hostile to both Christianity and Judaism.

In fact, two discoveries have now proved this theory to be entirely wrong. The first is the Dead Sea Scrolls. The second is the Chenoboskion papyri. At Chenoboskion, in middle Egypt, a jar containing bound volumes in various conditions of preservation was found by peasants about the same time as the Dead Sea Scrolls were first being discovered, though they only became known to scholars in 1948. The first scholar to recognize the extraordinary value of the documents, and to see that they derived from one of the almost completely lost early gnostic sects before the second century A.D., was a French scholar, Jean Doresse,[1] who was in Egypt on a fellowship for study of the Coptic monasteries, when this material was first brought to Cairo. He copied hundreds of pages of it, and his published volume, now available in English, remains the principal source of our knowledge.

Before this discovery, nothing was known about the early gnostics except what was preserved in the writings of the specialists in heresies, the so-called heresiographers, notably Irenaeus of Lyons (late second century), Hippolytus (early third century), and Epiphanius in the fourth century. (There were of course great numbers of original documents from the later gnostics.) In particular there were no documents known to derive from the followers of Simon Magus, the Simonians, or from the Nicolaitans, said by the early

[1] Jean Doresse, *The Secret Books of the Egyptian Gnostics*, New York, 1960.

41

church fathers to have been the followers of the deacon Nicolas (Acts 6), who was supposed to have become an apostate. Jean Doresse has now identified some Simonian fragments. The gnostics were believed by many scholars to be fairly orthodox Christians—the church fathers were said to have exaggerated their divergences. We now know that the church fathers were very reliable. They did not tell us everything by any means, but what they did tell us has been confirmed in large part by these new finds, and nothing of what they said has been shown to be wrong. This is just what we should expect, since they would have played directly into the hands of the gnostics, if they had misrepresented them. On the other side, there is no evidence today for pre-Christian gnosticism.

The New Testament therefore stands directly between the Essene literature from Qumran, composed largely in the first century B.C., and the early gnostic literature, composed in stages beginning with the middle decades of the first century A.D. Our new knowledge of the Essenes and gnostics has given us a number of clear points from which we can judge the historical position of the New Testament, and to which we can relate much of its phraseology and some of its teachings.

New Testament studies of the late 1940's and of subsequent years among the followers of Bultmann, like the critical views of twenty, thirty, and forty years ago, have been characterized by evolutionary historicism. This scheme spreads the New Testament books over a period of eighty to one hundred years, very roughly between 50 and 150 A.D., depending on the scholar and the amount of up-to-date evidence that he will accept. Within such a period there is plenty of room for the development of ideas, but it proceeds according to an arbitrary, unilinear system of evolution.

One such system is the Hegelian. Hegelian historicism proceeds according to rigorous dialectic, that is, first, a thesis, then a reaction, an antithesis, then a fusion of the two, a synthesis, which in turn becomes a thesis. This is the logical principle that Hegel thought would largely displace Aristotelian logic, and which for Marxists and Communists today is the basis of all historical thinking. For them the social sciences are as rigorous as the physical sciences, since they must proceed according to the strictest rules of dialectic materialism.

What new light has been thrown on specific areas of the New Testament by the discoveries at Qumran and Chenoboskion? The Johannine literature (that is, the Gospel of St. John and the three Epistles of John) used to be dated by many scholars somewhere between 100 and 170 A.D. (Today even radical scholars usually stop about 130 A.D.) These views are based on, and in turn become the bases of, the idea that the Johannine literature is completely non-Jewish, even anti-Jewish and thoroughly Greek in its background, and that it reflects a long period of evolution in the ideas and the theology both of Christ and of the apostles. Now, however, it appears that, while the Dead Sea Scrolls

43

illuminate much of the material in the Synoptic
Gospels, they provide far more parallels to the Johannine literature than to any other part of the New
Testament. Occasionally whole sentences are practi-
cally identical, and the two share numerous expressions
and points of view, as well as much imagery. (Of course
the theology is basically different: the one is thoroughly
Jewish, the other thoroughly Christian.) For example,
in both, as well as in scattered places in the Pauline
literature, and even in the Synoptic Gospels, we find
a contrasting of light and darkness, good and evil,
truth and falsehood. Early adumbrations of this appear
in the Old Testament, and more markedly in Zoroastrianism, but nowhere is it as clear-cut as in the
Dead Sea Scrolls, where, especially in the *Manual of
Discipline*, it is virtually a creed—the oldest creed yet
known in Judaeo-Christian literature.

In Zoroastrianism, the religion of the Iranians, there
were two co-existing, uncreated principles, the spirit
of light, good, and truth, and the spirit of evil, darkness,
and falsehood, the former of which would at the end of
time overcome the latter. In Essenism, both these
spirits are created by God, and their reflections are
found among good and evil men, good men being
possessed by a good spirit, evil men by an evil spirit.
In the New Testament the distinction between the two
is not so clear-cut, though it is relatively conspicuous
in Johannine literature as well as a very few other
passages such as the 5th chapter of Ephesians. In the
Lord's Prayer, for example, 'Lead us not into tempta-

tion' does not mean that God deliberately exposes people to temptation to see what will happen to them. *Peirasmos*, the term in question, refers to the conflict between the principles of good and evil—the almost never-ending battle for the individual soul and for mankind. St. Paul speaks of this warfare again and again, and if we understand the Lord's Prayer in the light of the Essene literature and particularly the Pauline writings, we must see here the testing which accompanies unremitting attacks by the spirits and forces of evil in this world.

The prologue to St. John's Gospel shows striking differences from, and striking similarities to, Qumran doctrine. The sentence: 'Without it was nothing made that was made', occurs almost word for word in the *Manual of Discipline*, though the subject there is the knowledge of God, i.e. right living, right thinking, and knowledge of Scripture. The Johannine term is, of course, 'Word'. Now there are admittedly Greek philosophical, especially Stoic, overtones to this term, but there is nothing in the prologue to suggest that anything other than Hebrew teachings is here referred to. An important new Aramaic targum of the Pentateuch has come to light in the Vatican Library, more recent than some of the Aramaic translations of the Bible among the Dead Sea Scrolls, but two or three centuries older than any previously known targum. In it the 'Word' of God appears as a surrogate for the name of God, Yahweh. This 'Word' is the creative and prophetic Word of God, as found in Genesis and the

Prophets and elsewhere in the Bible. It was substituted for direct references to God because man could not see God or come into direct contact with him except through his Word. Thus there is a crucial difference between the knowledge of God, which eventually led into gnosticism, and 'Word of God', which led to orthodox Christianity.

All the concrete arguments for a late date for the Johannine literature have now been dissipated, and Bultmann's attempts to discern an earlier and later form of the Gospel have proved to be entirely misleading, as both of his supposed redactions have similar Jewish background. The date which I personally prefer is the late 70's or early 80's, i.e. not more than thirty or forty years after the composition of the earliest Pauline epistles.

Paul tells us that he was a 'Pharisee of the Pharisees'. He was a disciple of one of the most famous Pharisee rabbis—Rabbi Gamaliel, who was in some ways the rabbinic figure whose teaching corresponded most closely to the apostolic teachings. Nevertheless we find in Pauline literature a number of parallels to Essene literature. We have already spoken of the war between the powers of light and darkness. For St. Paul this war is conducted both on the visible and on the invisible plane, both in the community at large and in the individual soul.

The Ephesian problem looks very different today. The new problems which face us have been vividly set forth in an article by K. G. Kuhn[1] on Ephesians 5.

[1] K. G. Kuhn, 'Der Epheserbrief im Lichte der Qumrantexte', *New Testament Studies*, 7, 1961.

The arguments against Pauline authorship have become very weak indeed, though it is difficult entirely to disprove arguments which are so hazy.

The 'mystery' of St. Paul has been put in a wholly new light by the discoveries at Qumran. Many scholars in the 90's and subsequent decades, followed by Bultmann and his school, maintained that the Pauline 'mystery' was taken over from the Greek mysteries, namely the mysteries of Dionysus, of Mithras, of Isis, the Eleusinian mysteries, etc. Years before the Dead Sea Scrolls were discovered, the late Arthur Darby Nock claimed in various places that there is nothing in common between the *mystērion* of the Pauline epistles and the *mystēria* of the Roman mysteries. This was plausible, but at the time it could not be convincingly proved. However, recently Father Raymond Brown[1] published his dissertation on the Semitic origin of the Pauline *mystērion*. He shows that it can in fact be traced back to the early books of the Old Testament, where the Hebrew *sôd* refers to the Heavenly Council, the assembly of God and his angels, and later to the decision taken by the Council. At this stage, it was identified with the Iranian *rāzā*, a word which first appears in Daniel, and was then taken over into the Essene literature in the same sense. In the intertestamental literature the word was translated *mystērion*. And now in the Hebrew and Aramaic Essene literature we find the word *rāz* used in exactly the same sense as

[1] Raymond E. Brown, S.S., 'The Qumran Scrolls and the Johannine Gospel and Epistles', *Catholic Biblical Quarterly*, 17, 1955.

that of the New Testament Greek equivalent, *mystērion*, except of course that St. Paul uses it with special reference to the mystery of salvation through Christ. Even the strange and still enigmatic 'mystery of iniquity' (Greek, *mystērion tēs anomias*) appears in Hebrew as *raz hap-pesha'*.

Thus Pauline terminology and thought are thoroughly Jewish, though probably not specifically Essene, since it is likely that the Pharisees had at this time similar ideas and phraseology (which soon disappeared in rabbinic times). In any case, Paul was probably in close association with the Essenes during those years of his life which he spent in Arabia, that is the Jordan Valley, Transjordan and the general area between the Arabian Desert and Palestine-Syria, the home of the Essenes.

There is no serious argument about the approximate date of most of the Pauline epistles, but the situation is different when we come to the Pastoral Epistles. Some scholars place them in the middle decades of the second century. Most of the arguments in favour of this date are stylistic, and are therefore not susceptible to proof, as there is nothing to tell us just what style or syntax would have been used by the amanuenses who wrote for St. Paul. The one concrete argument for a late date was the fact that before the discovery of the Dead Sea Scrolls no Hellenistic or Jewish prototype was known for the *episkopos*, the superintendent or overseer, whose character and requirements are stated in the Pastoral Epistles, where they certainly sound just like the requirements for a bishop in the early patristic literature of the late second century, when the institution of bishop emerges fully developed before our eyes. Hence, it was not unreasonable to suppose that since this institution presumably began from nothing, and gradually developed into the form which we find in the second century, therefore the letters to Timothy and Titus must come from this later period, and must in consequence be pseudonymous. However, we now have such a prototype, described particularly in the *Damascus Document* and the *Manual of Discipline*. In these documents we find the term *mebaqqer*, the ordinary Jewish-Aramaic and Hebrew word for overseer. As described, the functions and character of the *mebaqqer* are virtually identical with those of the Christian bishop of the second century, and of course with those of the *episkopos* of the Pastoral Epistles. Thus the one principal concrete argument against the Pauline date has vanished.

Luke-Acts has not been unaffected by our new materials. In my opinion Luke himself was a converted Jew. *Loukās*, the form in which his name appears in the New Testament, is the Greek form of an Aramaic *Lūqā*, which in turn is an abreviation of a Roman freedman's name, *Lucius*, *Lucanus* or *Lucianus*. Many Jews of that time were descendants of Jews who had been captured in the Judaean wars and sold into slavery in Italy and elsewhere. Many were freed and even taken into partnership by their previous masters. Such Jews are distinguishable by their Roman names in many

49

cases. A name of Latin origin might also be borne by a free Roman citizen, but the point is that it was given to slaves and retained by them when freed. It is unlikely that a non-Jew would use an Aramaic form of a Jewish freedman's Roman name. Both Mark and Luke bear such Roman freedman's names.

Dr. Paul Winter, who has made himself an authority on the Hebrew elements in the New Testament and on the Dead Sea Scrolls, has shown clearly that the three poems at the beginning of St. Luke's Gospel, the Magnificat, the Benedictus and the Nunc Dimittis, were actually written in Hebrew.[1] The same poetic style is found in the Dead Sea Scrolls. (Most of the material, of course, comes from the Old Testament.)

The Book of Acts shows that the early Christian community was organized almost throughout along the lines drawn by Essene organization, and in part probably according to the organization of the earliest Pharisees. Thus there are in the works of Luke indications of Jewish authorship, as well as good early Christian tradition.

In my opinion all the authors of the New Testament were Jews, and the New Testament has gained its Hellenistic elements largely through the Judaism of the pre-New-Testament period, when Jewish scholars such as Hillel introduced Greek logic, Greek rhetoric, and Greek hermeneutics into the exposition of the Hebrew Bible and the Jewish Law. So it is not

[1] P. Winter, 'The Proto-Source of Luke 1', *Novum Testamentum*, 1, 1956.

surprising that St. Paul's interpretation of the Old Testament follows the Greek hermeneutics of the Mishnah rather than the quite different type of interpretation found in the Essene commentaries on books of the Bible. It was only two generations later that St. Paul studied under Hillel's grandson in Jerusalem. He need have had no personal association with Greek scholars before his later life.

In the 1940's, the late Erwin Goodenough had already published his conclusions about the literature of the New Testament. Although our religious beliefs were quite different, I found myself in complete agreement with him in three important respects, since my study of the Dead Sea Scrolls. First, the books of the New Testament were composed during a period of possibly half a century, more likely thirty or forty years. Second, there is no trace of an evolution of doctrine within these books. (There were, of course, different reactions to the teachings of Christ, but these were contemporary, not successive.) Third, the whole New Testament bears witness to the early Christian belief in the risen Lord.[1]

[1] For a more detailed presentation of the material sketched above, see my essay in *The Teacher's Yoke: Studies in Memory of Henry Trantham*, Waco, 1964, pp. 27–41. Dr. C. S. Mann and I are planning a series of studies in this general area which will take us more deeply into the world of Jewish thought in the last two centuries B.C.